F A Q

of the Christian Faith

by

r. j. arthur
under shepherd, teacher, author, lecturer, student

_____
name

FAQ

of the Christian Faith

by

r. j. arthur
under shepherd, teacher, author, lecturer, student

Published by the P.A.C. of America

F.A.Q. of the Christian Faith

Copyright © February 02, 2014 by r. j. arthur. All rights reserved; however, all materials can and should be used as often as possible for spiritual gain, but may not be sold, reproduced, or used in any way for any financial gain.

ISBN: 978-1496059888

All scripture quotations, unless otherwise indicated, are taken from ESV Bible® (The Holy Bible, English Standard Version®). Copyright © 2001 by Crossway, a publishing ministry of Good News Publishers. Used by permission. All rights reserved.

Printed in the United States of America

This book is dedicated to my Father

(and to all my family)

Table of Context

Title Page .... **pages i - iv**

Dedication Page .... **page v**

Table of Context .... **page vii**

Preface .... **page ix**

How to Use this Study .... **page 1**

Session 1: *Aspects of Sin* .... **pages 2 - 7**

Session 2: *Effects of Sin* .... **pages 8 - 13**

Session 3: *Human Methods* .... **pages 14 - 19**

Session 4: *Trusting False gods* .... **pages 20 - 25**

Session 5: *The Way to God* .... **pages 26 - 31**

Session 6: *Being Born Again* .... **pages 32 - 37**

Session 7: *God's Speed* .... **pages 38 - 40**

Scriptural Footnotes

Preface

A Personal Note From The Author

The older I get the more I am learning the value of relationships. I suppose this may be a natural maturing process. But along with this natural progression, I believe I am spiritually maturing as well. Natural maturity comes through time and experiences. Spiritual maturity comes through knowing God and obedience.[1] Even though I started my spiritual journey over twenty-six years ago, I feel I am just beginning to grow. It seems like I am only now getting to know God and barely learning the basics on what it means to obey.

God often uses the physical things to reveal and teach us about the spiritual. For instance, to those who have received Jesus the Christ, to those who believe in His name, God calls them His children. Having an earthly father and being a son, along with being a father to children of my own, has given me a greater opportunity to understand what it means to have a spiritual relationship with a heavenly Father.

I have been so blessed to have been raised in a loving home and to have a wonderful immediate and extended family. This has laid a foundation, encouraged, and taught me more than what words may be able to describe. But I do not want to be misunderstood or misrepresent reality. Relationships are hard and are not without their challenges. I am not trying to paint a perfect "leave it to beaver" environment. My encouragement and lessons learned have often come through the dysfunctions, drama, and hardships that come with having close relationships. How sad if someone never had, or never takes, the opportunity to invest in getting to know their earthly family. What an even greater tragedy if someone never gets to know their heavenly Father or spiritual family.

This short story book is a reflection of my spiritual journey. It describes where I was, where I am, and where I am headed. We are all on this spiritual journey together. I am just one beggar that desires to tell others where I found some bread.

r. j. arthur

How To Use This Study

The FAQ of the Christian Faith has seven sections that progressively teach the gospel of Jesus the Christ. Each section contains the following:

- text that teaches various aspects of the gospel
- an illustration summarizing the teaching of the session
- step by step instructions how to draw the illustration
- questions pertaining to the session

Each section is called a session. Each session should take about twenty to thirty minutes to complete. Ideally, someone should try to read and complete one session every day in order to complete this FAQ workbook within one week.

After reading the text of a session the student should examine the corresponding illustration, draw out that day's illustration, and answer the questions. A student will need an 8.5" x 11" blank sheet of paper and pen or pencil. Drawing out each session is an important excise that should not be overlooked. Reading, seeing, creating, and reflecting are all important elements in comprehension.

Following each illustration is a series of questions pertaining to the session's text. The student should answer the questions pertaining to that day's session. The questions are designed to help in comprehending the main points of each session. The student will notice that the order of the questions directly corresponds to the session's text. For instance, question number one will deal with the first part of the text; question two will deal with the next part of the text; and so forth.

God has promised that His word will always do a work. His word is powerful and presently active. There are all kinds of reasons why people my want to understand the basics of Christianity. For those who desire to know God, He will reveal Himself clearly through His word.

Session 1: *Aspects of Sin*

In this chapter we consider three aspects of sin:
    1). What is sin?
    2). What is a sinner?
    3). Where did sin come from?

Most people would not consider it a compliment if they were called a sinner. In fact, people often use this word in a demeaning or derogatory manner. The Bible does not use this word in this kind of harsh demoralizing fashion. The Bible uses the term "sinner" to describe one's spiritual nature. Being a sinner simply means that someone has a sin nature; and by acting upon this nature they sin. It should be understood that one's nature is not produced by one's actions.[2] It is actually quite the opposite; one's nature produces one's actions. A person's actions actually identifies the origin of one's nature. When you sin, it is because you have a nature or propensity to sin. Rest assured, as a sinner, you are not alone. The Bible actually states that every single human that has ever lived is a sinner.[3] . As previously stated, being a sinner simply means that you have a nature or propensity to sin; but where did you get this sin nature?

To answer this question, we need to go all the way back to the beginning of time. In the beginning there was a holy and just God. He has always been, and always will be, a holy and perfect God.[4] He created everything: the heavens and earth, the plants, all the animals, and He also created the first humans – Adam and Eve.[5] He formed Adam's body from the dust of the ground. Then God breathed the breath of life into Adam's nostrils and he became a living being.[6] God created Adam with both physical and spiritual life. Since God is the creator, His nature is the standard by which everything else is compared. At this time, all of God's creation, including human beings, possessed and reflected God's holy and perfect nature.[7]

In Genesis, the first book of the Bible, we also learn that God placed Adam in a special garden in a place called Eden.[8] This was a place where Adam could have a perfect ideal relationship with God through his worship and obedience. There were all kinds of fruit trees

Session 1: *Aspects of Sin*

in this garden, including the tree of the knowledge of good and evil which was in the middle of the garden. God instructed Adam, "You are free to eat from any tree in the garden; but you must not eat from the tree of the knowledge of good and evil, for when you eat of it you will surely die."[9] God provided for Adam's every need so Adam could reflect God's nature in his relationship with his Creator.[10]

God also created Eve with both a physical and spiritual life.[11] She received the same instructions about the forbidden fruit in the middle of the garden. A serpent (i.e. Satan) approached her and tried to convince her to eat the fruit from the tree of the knowledge of good and evil. The first four words the Devil said to humanity was, "Did God actually say..?" Satan, even to this very day, constantly tries to get people to doubt or question their understanding of God's word. Satan asked Eve, "Did God actually say, 'You shall not eat of any tree in the garden'?" Eve answered him, "We may eat fruit from the trees in the garden, but God did say, 'You must not eat fruit from the tree that is in the middle of the garden, and you must not touch it, or you will die.'"[12] Did you notice that Eve did not exactly understand or say what God had told Adam? This gave the serpent the foothold he needed in order to deceive and manipulate her.

Tragically, Satan was successful in deceiving Eve, convincing her that she misunderstood what God had said, so she ate the fruit from the tree of the knowledge of good and evil. After Eve ate the forbidden fruit she also gave some to her husband who was with her, and he also ate.[13] When this happened, for the very first time, sin entered the world through Adam's act of disobeying God's Word.[14] All of God's creation, not just Adam and Eve, was affected. God's creation no longer perfectly reflected God's nature and character. It was now tainted by what Adam had done. The Creator's desired relationship with Adam was altered due to his disobedience, or what the Bible calls sin. Sin is simply missing the mark. This is any action that does not perfectly reflect the nature of God.[15] Adam and Eve had become sinners (i.e. they had acquired a sin nature). Their actions have a direct effect on all of creation.

Session 1: *Aspects of Sin*

In summary, sin is any thought, word, or deed that does not reflect the character or nature of God. This occurs anytime someone does not obey God's word perfectly.[16] A sinner is a person who has the nature to sin; that is, they reflect the nature of Satan rather than the nature of God. The author or originator of sin is Satan. Lucifer was the most beautiful angelic created being. The dilemma for Lucifer was that He had pride. He rejected God and wanted humanity to worship him instead of God.[17] He relied on himself instead of trusting in God. This caused the most beautiful angel to fall from his lofty prestigious position.[18] We commonly know this angel by the name of Satan, the Devil, the Adversary, ruler of this world, etc. Have you ever had pride? Have you ever wanted the praise of men instead of having men praise God? Have you ever rejected God and relied on your abilities instead of trusting God? Of course you have! Because a sinner possesses the nature of Satan. As we will see in the next chapter, as a result of Adam's sin, every single person is a sinner.

The following diagram illustrates the summary of this chapter:

- The line drawn across the folded paper represents an eternal timeline. A holy and just God has no beginning and no end.

- The word "God" on the left side of the page represents the one true holy God of the Bible.

- The male stick figure on the right represents Adam.

- The female stick figure on the right represents Eve.

- The "P" above the stick figures represents their physical life.

- The "S" above the stick figures represents their spiritual life.

- The word "sin" represents the sin of Adam that affected all of creation.

Session 1: *Aspects of Sin*

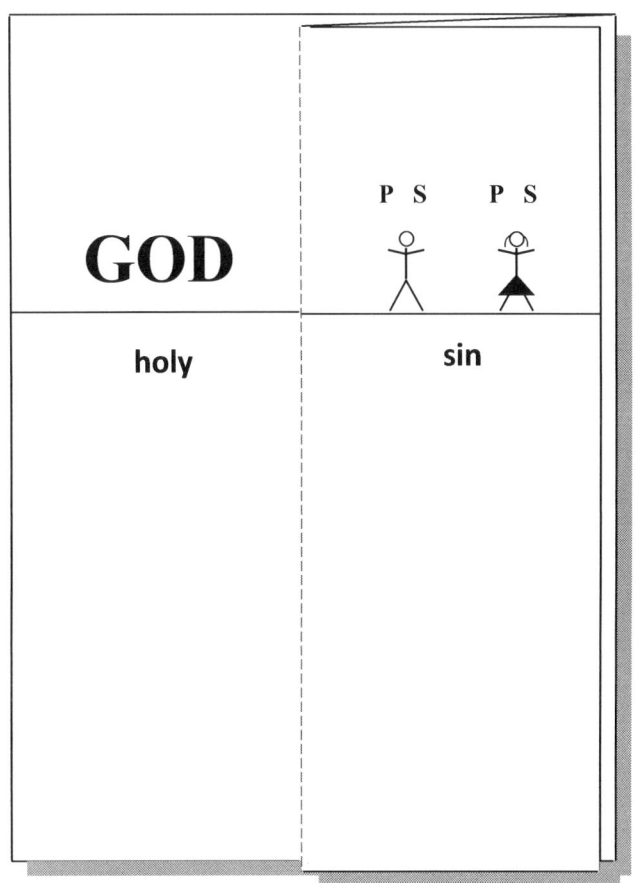

Session 1: *Aspects of Sin*

Drawing Session 1: *Aspects of Sin*

Fold the right side of a piece of paper (preferably 8½" by 11") in half over the left side (i.e. as seen in letter "A" below).

Fold just the back half of the paper in half again (i.e. letter "B" below).

The paper should now look like letter "C" below.

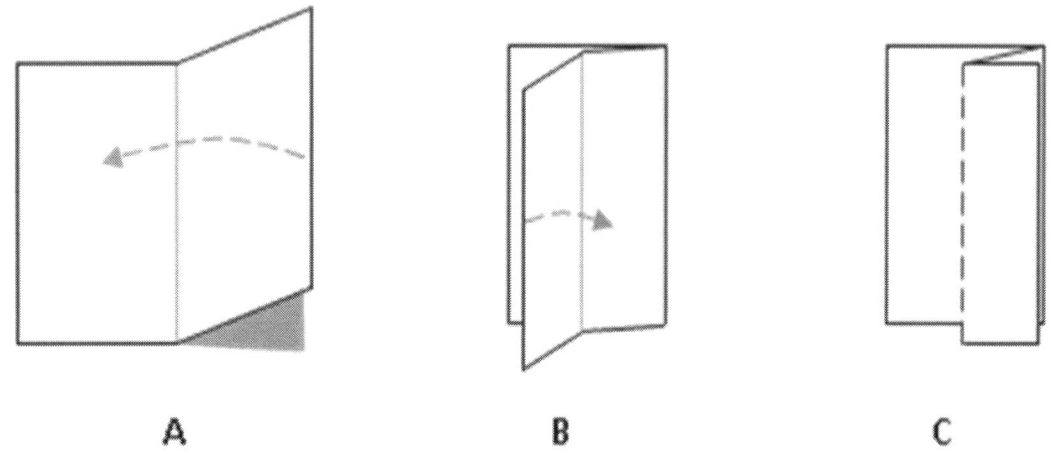

Draw a horizontal line about a third the way down across the folded piece of paper. Write "**GOD**" above line on left and "**holy**" under line.

Draw a man stick figure above line on the right with a "**P**" (i.e. for physical life) and an "**S**" (i.e. for spiritual life) above the stick figure.

Draw a woman stick figure next to the man with "**P**" and "**S**" above.

Write "**sin**" under the stick figure to represent their disobedience to God's word.

Session 1: *Aspects of Sin*

Questions for Session 1: *Aspects of Sin*

1.0 **According to the Bible, how many people are sinners?** *The Bible actually states that every single human that has ever lived is a sinner (Romans 3:23 with 5:12, 18-19). As we will see in the next chapter, as a result of Adam's sin, every single person is a sinner (first and last paragraph).*

2.0 **What is God's nature like?** *He has always been, and always will be, a holy and perfect God (second paragraph, Lev 11:44-45).*

3.1 **What did God tell Adam that he was allowed to do?** *"You are free to eat from any tree in the garden..." (third paragraph, Genesis 2:16).*

3.2 **What did God tell Adam that he was not allowed to do?** *"...but you must not eat from the tree of the knowledge of good and evil..." (third paragraph, Genesis 2:17).*

3.3 **What did God tell Adam would happen if he did the very thing that God told him not to do?** *"...for when you eat of it you will surely die." (third paragraph, Genesis 2:17).*

3.4 **Why did Eve eat the fruit from the tree of knowledge of good and evil?** *Tragically, Satan was successful in deceiving Eve, convincing her that she misunderstood what God had said (fifth paragraph Genesis 3:1-6).*

3.5 **Who gave the forbidden fruit to Adam?** *After Eve ate the forbidden fruit she also gave some to her husband who was with her, and he also ate (fifth paragraph, Genesis 3:6-7).*

4.0 **What is sin?** *Sin is any thought, word, or deed that does not reflect the character or nature of God. This occurs anytime someone does not obey God's word perfectly (last paragraph, Romans 14:23).*

Session 2: *Effects of Sin*

In this chapter we will explore three effects of sin:
1). What effect did Adam's sin have on the spiritual world?
2). What effect did Adam's sin have on the physical world?
3). What effect did Adam's sin personally have on you?

God had previously established the penalty for disobeying His word. The consequence of Adam's sin was death.[19] Since God is a holy and just God, He is always true to His word. God, being true to His word, immediately imposed the penalty of death. God always keeps His word – this is part of His nature![20]

There are two aspects of death, each corresponding to the two aspects of man – physical death and spiritual death.[21] Death simply means separation. In physical death, the soul is separated from the physical body. Without the soul, the body ceases to function.[22] In spiritual death, the soul is separated from God (i.e. the source of life). As God promised, when Adam and Eve ate the fruit from the tree of knowledge of good and evil, Adam and Eve immediately spiritually died. This means they became spiritually dead; that is, separated from God! It was just as though a huge bottomless pit had opened between God and mankind. God is on one side and mankind completely spiritually isolated from God on the other. Man became sinful and therefore became separated from their holy Creator.

When man brought sin into the world by disobeying God's Word, Adam and Eve acquired a sin nature. Their thoughts, words, and actions became a reflection of their new spiritual father, Satan, instead of a reflection of their Creator God.[23] In fact, mankind became a prisoner or enslaved to sin.[24] The only choice they now possessed was to sin. Their sin nature is what now dictated their actions. When they acquired a sin nature, as God had promised, mankind died spiritually. Adam and Eve became slaves to sin and were no longer able to fulfill their intended purpose; which was, to glorify God through obedience within a perfect ideal relationship with their Creator.

Session 2: *Effects of Sin*

After Adam and Eve had sinned against God, they were ejected from the garden in Eden.[25] Not only did they immediately spiritually die, they began to physically die as well. Since God gave Adam responsibility over all of creation, all of creation was affected by his sin. Things began to change. There was now pestilence, diseases, and eventually physical death.[26] Everything began to degenerate. This is evident to this day. Are things improving? Is the gene pool getting more pure or more diluted? Are we acquiring more new species or are we losing species? It is estimated (depending on which science camp you fall in) there are between 2000 up to 100,000 species going extinct every single year. The point is, when Adam and Eve sinned and sin entered all of creation, this not only had an immediate effect on their spiritual condition, but it altered all of the physical creation as well.

Adam and Eve lived what we might consider a 'normal' life. Though they were physically dying, they lived to be very old and had many children, who had many children, and so on. All the people from Adam and Eve to you and me have inherited some common human characteristics from Adam. We have ten fingers, ten toes, hair, two eyes, two ears, etc. Along with these characteristics, we also all inherited a human nature; the same type of nature as possessed by Adam. All of us were physically born into this world with a sin nature, which our "father" Adam acquired when he disobeyed God in the garden in Eden. This sin nature has been inherited and passed on from one generation to the next. You might say, "It is in our jeans" (ha ha, an intentional pun on genes).

Since we all have inherited and entered this world with the same sin nature as Adam and Eve, we also enter the world spiritually separated from God as a slave to sin (i.e. spiritually dead). We have an everlasting soul but it is spiritually dead; that is, separated from God. Not only are we spiritually dead, we are all physically dying. We are all in an environment that is self-destructive and degenerating. We have

9

Session 2: *Effects of Sin*

all inherited a sin nature, as well as other human characteristics, but we cannot inherit spiritual life through our parents. We must receive spiritual life from God. Up to this point, things may seem very grim and negative. Keep reading... it eventually gets mind-blowingly better.

In Summary, the Bible says sin ultimately produces death (i.e. separation, destruction, degeneration, etc.). The following diagram illustrates the summary of this chapter:

- Putting an "X" through the "S" above each stick figure represents the spiritual death Adam and Eve immediately experienced when Adam disobeyed and sinned against God. This also represents the type of nature they now both possessed; that is, a sin nature.

- Opening up the folded piece of paper and drawing lines down each side, represents the spiritual separation that every human being experiences due to inheriting a sin nature from Adam.

- Writing "Physical Birth" on the top right side represents the only type of life that can be produced by humanity. We can only pass on physical life but we cannot give spiritual life.

- Drawing additional stick figures below the original two stick figures, represents the all the generations from Adam and Eve to you and me. Notice that all these generations are born with physical life, but none of them can be born with spiritual life. All the generations from Adam and Eve to you and me have been born spiritually separated from God.

Session 2: *Effects of Sin*

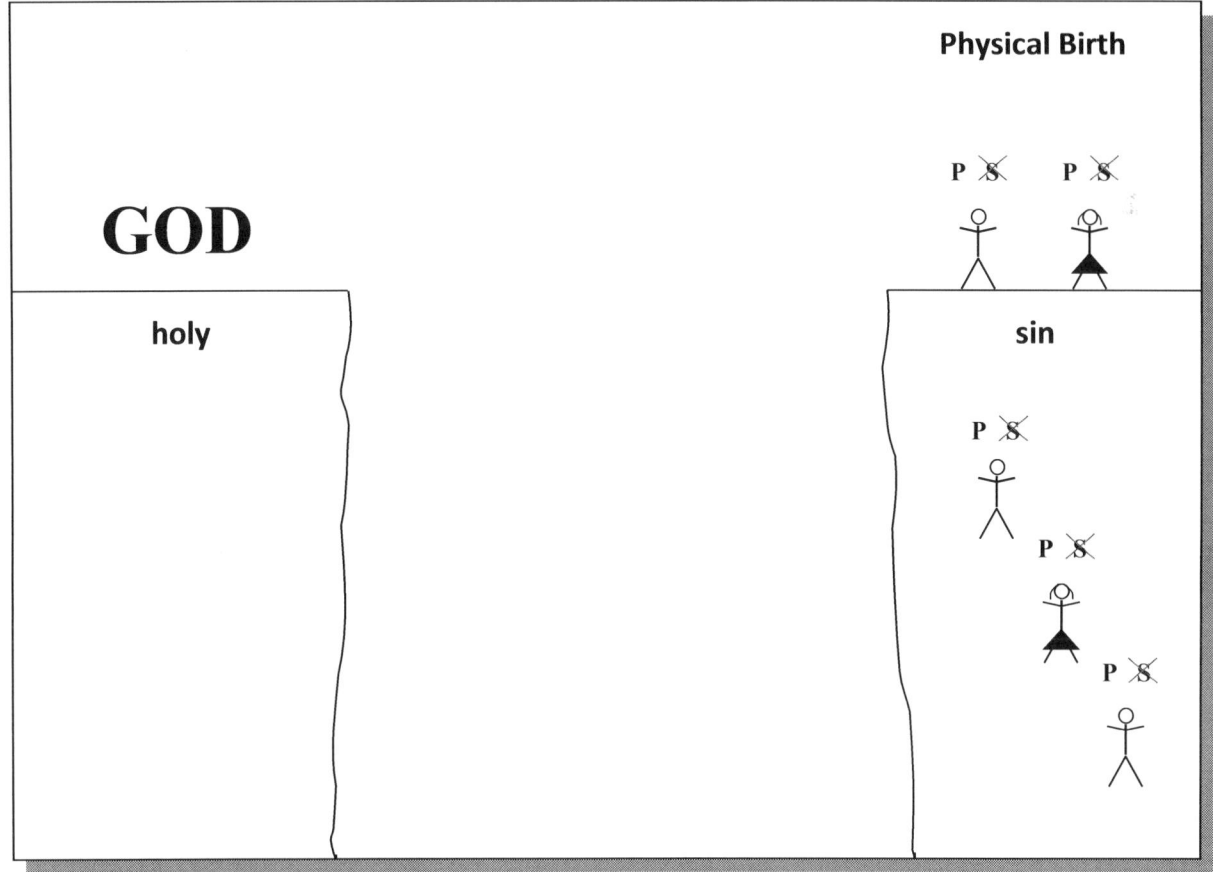

Session 2: *Effects of Sin*

Drawing Session 2: *Effects of Sin*

Write an "**X**" through the "**S**" above each stick figure to represent the spiritual death Adam and Eve immediately experienced when they disobeyed and sinned against God. This also represents the type of nature they now both possessed; that is, a sin nature.

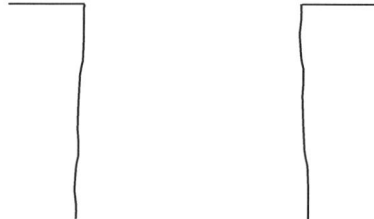

Opening up the folded piece of paper and drawing lines down each side, represents the spiritual separation (i.e. spiritual death) that every human experiences due to inheriting a sin nature from Adam.

Write "**Physical Birth**" on the top right side to represent the only type of life that can be produced by humanity. We can only pass on physical life but we cannot give spiritual life.

Physical Birth

Drawing additional stick figures below the original two stick figures, represents all the generations from Adam and Eve to you and me. Notice that all these generations are born with physical life, but none of them can be physically born with spiritual life. All the generations from Adam and Eve to you and me have been physically born spiritually separated from God.

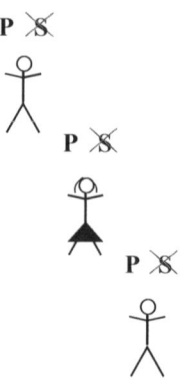

Session 2: *Effects of Sin*

Questions for Session 2: *Effects of Sin*

1.0 What immediately happened when Adam and Eve disobeyed God's word (i.e. sinned)? *The consequence of Adam's sin was death (first paragraph, Romans 5:12 with Romans 6:23).*

2.1 What does it mean to die physically? *In physical death, the soul is separated from the physical body. Without the soul, the body ceases to function (second paragraph, James 2:26).*

2.2 What does it mean to die spiritually? *In spiritual death, the soul is separated from God (second paragraph, Revelation 20:14).*

3.0 After Adam sinned, what nature did Adam and Eve inherit? *When man brought sin into the world by disobeying God's Word, Adam and Eve acquired a sin nature (third paragraph)*

4.0 What are some consequences due to Adam disobeying God's word (i.e. sinning)? *Adam and Eve acquired a sin nature; they became a slave to sin; they died spiritually; they could no longer fulfill their intended purpose; they were ejected from the presence of God in the garden; they began to die physically; there was now pestilence, diseases, and eventually physical death; all of creation began to deteriorate (third and fourth paragraph).*

5.0 When parents have a sin nature, what kind of nature will their children inherit? *A sin nature (fifth and sixth paragraph, Romans 5:12, 18).*

6.0 **(True)** or **False.** When an innocent little baby is physically born, they are born spiritually dead as a sinner; that is, spiritually separated from God. *(fifth and sixth paragraph, Romans 5:12, 18).*

Session 3: *Human Methods*

In this chapter we will explore:
1). How does humanity try to get to God?
2). What are four common examples of human efforts trying to obtain spiritual life?

There are several ways that humanity tries to restore their broken relationship with God. People often try to get to God through their own efforts by building what we will call "human bridges." The sin nature naturally causes us to create and do things on our own instead of relying and trusting in God. We will even try to accomplish spirituality through our carnal ability which is motivated by our sin nature. It is a common misconception that if we try to do spiritual things then we will become spiritual. Or if we try to look and act spiritual then we will become spiritual. This makes perfect sense according to our sin nature, but it is not consistent with God's nature. To clarify this point, let's consider some common "bridges" people often attempt to build.

One of the bridges people try to build is "Good Works." People often believe if they do things that appear to be God-like or good, then they will be accepted by God. People commonly believe that if they do more good things than bad, then God will reward the good and forget about or overlook the bad. Unfortunately, God is not impressed with our good works. In fact, the Bible says our good deeds are as impressive to God as a pile of filthy disgusting used dirty rags.[27] All goodness has its origin with God, not with sinful man. Our attempts of acting good fall far short of spanning the chasm of our spiritual separation from God. Good works cannot deliver us from spiritual death over to spiritual life.

"Prayer" is another bridge people often rely on to spiritually reunite them to God. Many people believe that they must sincerely ask God to forgive their sins or say some kind of prayer for their relationship with God to be restored. It is almost if God were viewed as a genie in a magic bottle. If we ask God, then God will hop to and grant our request. Prayer is a way in which someone who has a restored

Session 3: *Human Methods*

relationship with God can communicate with their Creator; however, there is not any prayer that will restore a broken relationship, or bridge the gap, between mankind and God.

There are many people sitting in the pews of prominent, and not so prominent, churches that are trusting in church membership and/or attending "Church Gatherings" to bridge the gap between God and mankind. The Bible teaches that everyone who has had their relationship with God restored belong, or are a part of, the true church known as the ecclesia (i.e. called out ones). This is a spiritual group that God assembles, not a physical group that regularly has regular meetings and events. There is no group or regular assembly of people we can join that will restore our broken relationship with God. "Going to church" cannot reconcile man to God.

Although there are many bridges people attempt to build to try and reach God, for purposes of this illustration, the last bridge we will consider is the "Baptism" bridge. The word baptize is a transliterated word from the Koiné Greek language. The word simply means to be so immersed or saturated with something that you are identified with it. For instance, someone can be baptized in fear; meaning, they are so full of fear that if you look at them you would recognize that they are scared to death. Or someone could be baptized in love. We have all seen those couples that are oozing with love as they gaze into each other's eyes (Oh, yuck). Usually people reference baptism with being immersed or saturated with water. If one is relying on this baptism to bridge their relationship with God, they are simply all wet. Baptism with water can never restore one's relationship with God.

Though all these bridges fall far short in bridging the relational gap between mankind and God, it must be made perfectly clear that each of the so called bridges we discussed can have a very important place in our spiritual life. Spiritual actions flow out of spiritual people. But simply doing spiritual actions does not make someone spiritual. Humans put value on the outward actions, but God looks on the

Session 3: *Human Methods*

heart.[28] The dilemma for mankind is the heart. We need God to give us a new heart (i.e. new nature), and then spiritual actions will flow out of that new nature. No bridge humanity tries to build has the ability to give spiritual life! It is only after someone has been given spiritual life that spiritual actions can fulfill their designed purpose.

In summary, it is human nature to try and do things to reconcile the broken relationship between God and mankind. There are all kinds of religions and spiritual activities that mankind practices in order to try to become more spiritual. No action mankind does can bridge the relational gap between man and God.

The following diagram illustrates the summary of this chapter:

- The first platform or "bridge" is "Good Works." As can be seen in the illustration, the bridge of good works falls far short of bridging the gap between mankind and God.

- The next bridge is "Prayer." Simply asking, begging, or talking to God can never restore one's broken spiritual relationship to God. Individuals need a new heart. Putting one's hope in prayer is not the way to gain a new heart or nature.

- The next bridge is "Church Gatherings." Many well intended people put an emphasis on going to an event they call "church" or joining an exclusive "membership." From Genesis through Revelation, the Bible records man's failed attempts to please or gain access to God through various organized events.

- Though there are many spiritual things people try to do to please God in order to restore their broken relationship, for our purposes the last bridge is "Baptism." Again, many well intended people have trusted that they have a healthy relationship with God because they were immersed or saturated with water. There is no amount of water that can restore the broken spiritual relationship between humanity and God.

Session 3: *Human Methods*

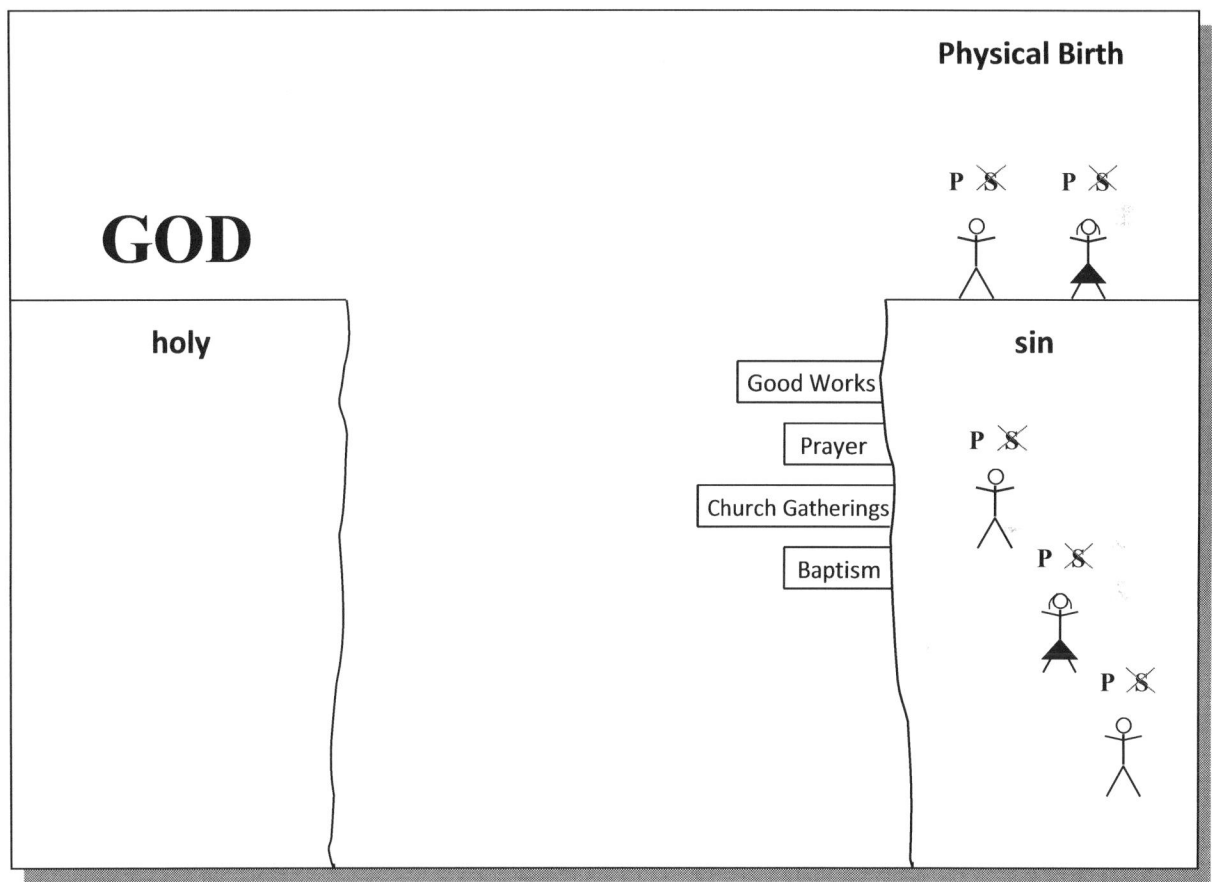

Session 3: *Human Methods*

Drawing Session 3: *Human Methods*

Draw the "Good Works" bridge and write **"Good Works"** inside of it

Draw the "Prayer" bridge and write **"Prayer"** inside of it

Draw the "Church Gatherings" bridge and write **"Church Gatherings"** inside of it

Draw the "baptism" bridge and write **"Baptism"** inside of it

Session 3: *Human Methods*

Questions for Session 3: *Human Methods*

1.0 **(True)** or **False.** If someone desires to be spiritual then they must look and act spiritual. *It is a common misconception that if we do spiritual things then we will become spiritual; or If we try to look and act spiritual then we will become spiritual (first paragraph, Luke 20:45-47). Spiritual actions flow out of spiritual people. But simply doing spiritual actions does not make someone spiritual. Humans put value on the outward actions, but God looks on the heart (sixth paragraph, 1 Sam 16:7).*

2.0 Compared to the goodness of God, what does the bible say our good works (i.e. good deeds) are like? *The Bible says our good deeds are as impressive to God as a pile of filthy disgusting used dirty rags (second paragraph, Isaiah 64:6).*

3.0 **True** or **(False)** In order for people to restore their broken relationship with God, they must earnestly pray for God to forgive them of their sins. *Prayer is a way in which someone who has a restored relationship with God can communicate with their Creator; however, there is not any prayer that will restore a broken relationship, or bridge the gap, between mankind and God (third paragraph).*

4.0 What is the true church here on earth? *The Bible teaches that everyone who has had their relationship with God restored belong, or are a part of, the true church known as the ecclesia (i.e. called out ones). This is a spiritual group that God assembles, not a physical group that regularly has regular meetings and events (fourth paragraph, Matthew 6:18; 1 Corinthians 12:13 with Colossians 1:18).*

5.0 What does the word "baptize" mean? *The word baptize is a transliterated word from the Koiné Greek language. The word simply means to be so immersed or saturated with something that you are identified with it (fifth paragraph).*

6.0 **True** or **(False)** There is no spiritual value in doing spiritual things. *Though all these bridges fall far short in bridging the relational gap between mankind and God, it must be made perfectly clear that each of the so called bridges we discussed can have a very important place in our spiritual life (sixth paragraph).*

Session 4: *Trusting False gods*

In this chapter we will explore:
    1). Does God exist?
    2). What is a false god?
    3). What are the consequences of trusting in a false god?

Before someone could even try to reconcile their spiritual relationship with God, one must acknowledge and understand the reality or existence of God. The Bible never tries to prove God's existence. The Bible simply states the fact, "In the beginning God created…" The Bible states that God has clearly shown His eternal power and divine nature through creation; but, mankind will often not honor Him as God or even acknowledge Him. People all too often turn their hearts away from God instead of pursuing a relationship with Him. In conclusion of this thought, the Bible says men are without any excuses because they should have known better, even if for no other reason, because creation reveals the evidence of God.[29]

A friend recently told me an interesting story: There were two close friends that took very different paths in their youth. One became a devout believer in God, and the other an atheist. The atheist would claim that there is no evidence of God while the believer proclaimed that, at the very least, creation demonstrates the existence of God. The atheist became a devoted scientist who specialized in astronomy and said all of creation appeared by chance happenings. For his birthday, the believer had one of his engineering friends design and build a very precise working scale model of our solar system. All the planets were rotating at just the right speeds as they orbited the sun in their exact elliptical paths and velocities. The atheist was delighted with his gift. As he explored this replica of the universe, he was amazed at the accuracy and precision of the scale model. In complete astonishment the atheist asked, "Who was the engineer who designed and created this beautiful scale model. His believing friend simply replied, "No one, it just appeared by chance over billions of years. I simply discovered it

Session 4: *Trusting False gods*

and gave it to you." God is a revealing Creator who can be seen and known. He desires to have a personal relationship with His creation.

As long as we are separated from God, our human devices and attempts to reach Him will be to no avail. Realizing that there is a God is perhaps the first step in pursuing reconciliation. It is only after someone comes to the realization that a personal revealing Creator actually exists, that they can pursue getting to know Him. Unfortunately, even after this realization, people will often be led astray by creating faulty systems or religions. These faulty systems or religions becomes their false faith in a false god. This is the god in which they are trusting. In fact, everyone has faith in something whether they believe in God or not. Even the atheist has faith that there is no true faith. Our present culture is plagued with relativism. The only absolute truth that the relative thinker adopts is that there is absolutely no such thing as absolute truth. And they are absolutely sure that there is no absolute truth. Since there is only one true God, then there is only one true faith. Everyone has a god. Whatever people are truly trusting or believing in becomes their god.

The tragedy is that when one's physical life on this earth comes to an end, and if they are still separated from God (i.e. spiritually dead) because of having trusted in erroneous ways of restoring their relationship with God, they will remain in that state forever. They will be separated from God forever in a place often referred to as hell (i.e. hades, the second death, lake of fire, etc.). The Bible calls this the second death because it is not the first death. The first death is the physical death, whereas the second death references spiritual death. And do you know how the Bible describes spiritual death? The second death is the complete separation from God in total darkness and isolation, under perpetual judgment and torment, without hope, forever and ever and ever![30] It is impossible for anyone to even begin to imagine how utterly horrible it is to be completely and permanently separated from God. Nor can words describe the misery that will be

Session 4: *Trusting False gods*

experienced by mind, soul, and body. Imagine spending forever in such a place apart from God. And the saddest reality is that this is totally unnecessary!

It is not God's desire that any person should be separated from Him in such a place.[31] It is His desire that every person would cross the chasm of separation and be united with Him in a perfect restored eternal relationship. God desires that every person should have spiritual life and spend eternity in a perfect relationship with Him. Because of His immeasurable love for us, His great mercy and amazing grace, God has provided a way for us to cross the great chasm separating mankind from God. God was under no obligation to do this. It is only out of His loving nature that God has provided a way for our relationship to be perfectly restored.[32]

In summary, there is only one true God and therefore only one absolute truth and only one true faith. God's existence is evident through creation. No one has any excuses for denying the existence of God. No one has any excuse for not pursuing a relationship with their Creator. The Bible says, "The fool says in his heart, 'There is no God.' They are corrupt, they do abominable deeds, there is none who does good."[33] In actuality, whether they realize it or not, whatever people are trusting in is their god. This could be science, one's own intellect, materialism, false religions, the bridges in our diagram, etc. There are eternal consequences in having faith in anything or anyone other than the one true God. If someone experiences the first death without having true faith in the one true God, they will experience the second death (i.e. spiritual death).

The following diagram illustrates the summary of this chapter:

- All the arrows going down from the "bridges" represent people having faith in false gods when they die.

- Writing the word "Hell" at the end of these arrows represents the second death (i.e. spiritual death).

Session 4: *Trusting False gods*

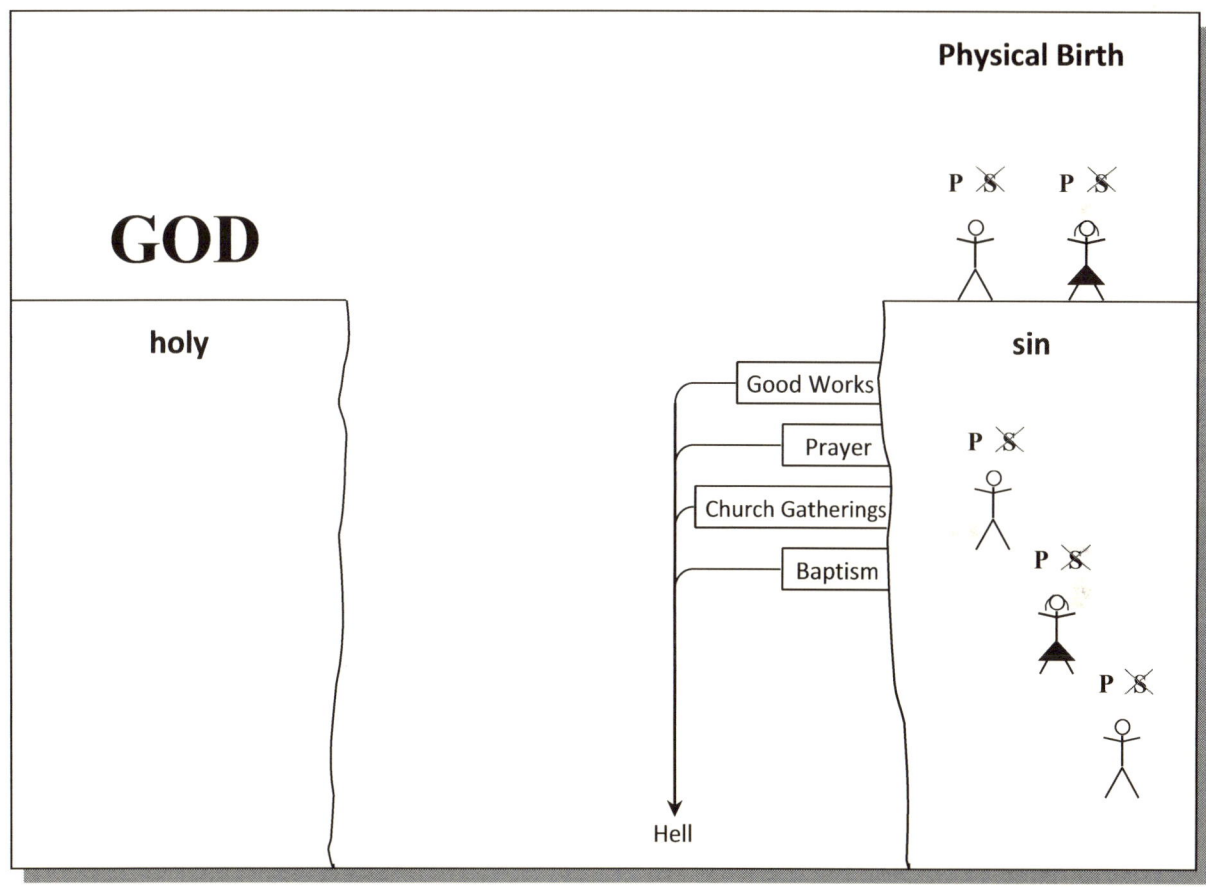

Session 4: *Trusting False gods*

Drawing Session 4: *Trusting False gods*

Draw the arrows downward from the human bridges.

Write the word "**Hell**" at the bottom of the arrow. This word represents the second death and the eternal consequences in having faith in anything or anyone other than the one true God.

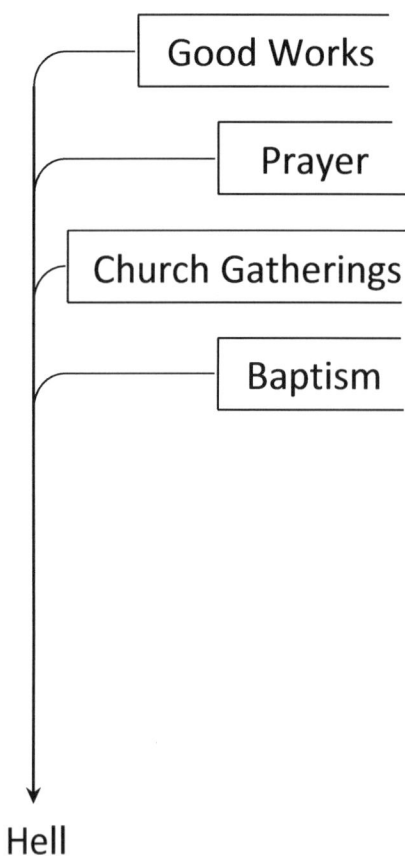

Session 4: *Trusting False gods*

Questions for Session 4: *Trusting False gods*

1.0 **What is at least one thing that clearly shows God's invisible attributes; namely, his eternal power and divine nature?** *"For what can be known about God is plain to [mankind], because God has shown it to them. For his invisible attributes, namely, his eternal power and divine nature, have been clearly perceived, ever since the creation of the world, in the things that have been made. So they are without excuse" (Romans 1:19-20).*

2.0 **(True) or False. Everyone believes in a god.** *Whatever people are trusting or believing in becomes their god (third paragraph). The word god, in a generic sense, is someone or something that dominates: someone or something that is so important that it takes over somebody's life.*

3.0 **(True) or False. Since there is only one true God, there is only one absolute truth and only one true faith.** *Since there is only one true God, then there is only one true faith (third paragraph). There are eternal consequences in having faith in anything or anyone other than the one true God (last paragraph).*

4.0 **Describe the first death and the second death.** *Death means separation. Death means separation. The first death is the soul separating from the body (i.e. physical death). The second death is the person being separated from God; that is spiritual death (fourth and last paragraph, Revelation 20:6, 14; 21:8).*

5.0 **What is God's desire concerning His relationship with mankind?** *It is His desire that every person would cross the chasm of separation and be united with Him in a perfect restored eternal relationship (fifth paragraph, 1 Timothy 2:3-4).*

6.0 **According to the Bible, what does the fool say in his heart and how is a fool described?** *"The fool says in his heart, 'There is no God.' They are corrupt, they do abominable deeds, there is none who does good" (last paragraph, Psalm 14:1).*

25

Session 5: *The Way to God*

In this chapter we will explore:
1). Who is the way, the truth, and the life?
2). What has Jesus done in order to restore mankind to God?
3). Why would such a good man like Jesus die for a sinner like me?

Do you know the way to God? Jesus the Christ said, "I am the way, and the truth, and the life. No one comes to the Father except through me."[34] Jesus did not say that good works, prayer, church gatherings, baptism, or anything else is the way. He said: "I am *the way*." God the Son was sent by God the Father into this world to become The Bridge between mankind and God. He is the only way by which we may cross the spiritual chasm created by sin. Sin produces spiritual death but God's love through Jesus the Christ produces spiritual life. "For God so loved the world, that he gave his only Son, that whoever believes in him should not perish but have eternal life."[35] By placing faith in Jesus as the only true way, one is placing faith in the one true God.

Not only did Jesus say He is the only way, Jesus also stated that there are no exceptions. He said that *no one* can come to God except through Him. There are no exceptions! We may not like it. We may not think this is fair, but this is the reality. Accepting or trusting in anything but Jesus will lead to the second death. This is the truth. Jesus said He is the way and *the truth*. There is only one Jesus and there is only one truth. Knowing the truth will set a person free.[36] The truth will free the individual who is enslaved by sin through their sin nature. Jesus the Christ is the way and the truth.

Jesus also said He is *the life*. Trusting in Him alone will give spiritual life. Through faith in Christ, an individual will cross over from spiritual death to spiritual life. And Jesus does not give just any kind of life; he gives eternal life. The idea behind eternal life is not just simply the longevity of life, but the quality of life.[37] The spiritual life obtained

Session 5: *The Way to God*

through faith in Jesus is like no other. Christ gives an abundant life of the highest quality.[38] It is infinite, beyond description, provides peace that is surpasses all understanding; it is eternal life. Jesus is the way, the truth, and the life.

What did Jesus Christ actually do to become this bridge? By shedding His blood and dying upon the cross, being buried in the grave, and resurrected the third day according to the scriptures, Jesus became the life-giving savior for mankind.[39] God the Son (i.e. Jesus the Christ) is always in perfect harmonious fellowship with God the Father.[40] His entire existence is purposed to obey the Father in order to reveal the Father for the Father's glory. Glorifying God the Father is the core essence of Jesus' Personhood.[41] Though the physical agony of enduring an execution by means of crucifixion was horrific, there was something far worse Jesus endured. He pleaded with the Father, if it were at all possible (and with God all things are possible) for the Father to not ask Him to go to the cross.[42] Again, Jesus was not afraid of the physical pain (though I am sure he wasn't looking forward to it). He could not bear to be separated from His Father. Anything but that! None the less, Jesus conceded His own will to be obedient to the will of the Father. He obediently went to the cross and took on the sin of the world.[43] He experienced the full wrath of God. He experienced the full brunt of the second death multiplied by the number of humans that will ever live. Wow!

I am constantly amazed that the Father would have Jesus the Christ die for me. I can see if someone were to take a bullet for a good or important man, but to give your life for a sinner who did not even know or acknowledge God? Not only am I completely wretched, but Jesus is as perfect as God is perfect.[44] Jesus the Christ is God Himself who became flesh being born in the likeness of man.[45] He was born of a virgin.[46] He did not have a sin nature; but rather, He has the nature of

Session 5: *The Way to God*

His heavenly Father (i.e. God). The Bible describes God's perfection as righteous. Every sinner is unrighteous. Christ is righteous (i.e. without sin) and therefore did not deserve to die, but He died in our place (i.e. the unrighteous). "For Christ also suffered once for sins, the righteous for the unrighteous, that he might bring us to God."[47] "For one will scarcely die for a righteous person—though perhaps for a good person one would dare even to die— but God shows his love for us in that while we were still sinners, Christ died for us."[48]

In summary, much like Adam's act of disobedience had a negative spiritual effect, Jesus' act of obedience has a positive spiritual effect. He is the way, the truth, and the life. No one comes to God the Father apart from Him. The following diagram illustrates the summary of this chapter:

- The cross with Jesus the Christ written in the middle represents that Jesus is the way, the truth, and the life. He is The Bridge that God the Father has provided so mankind can cross over from spiritual death to spiritual life.

- John 14:6. "Jesus said to him, 'I am the way, and the truth, and the life. No one comes to the Father except through me.'"

- John 3:16. "For God so loved the world, that he gave his only Son, that whoever believes in him should not perish but have eternal life."

- 1st Peter 3:18a. "For Christ also suffered once for sins, the righteous for the unrighteous, that he might bring us to God…"

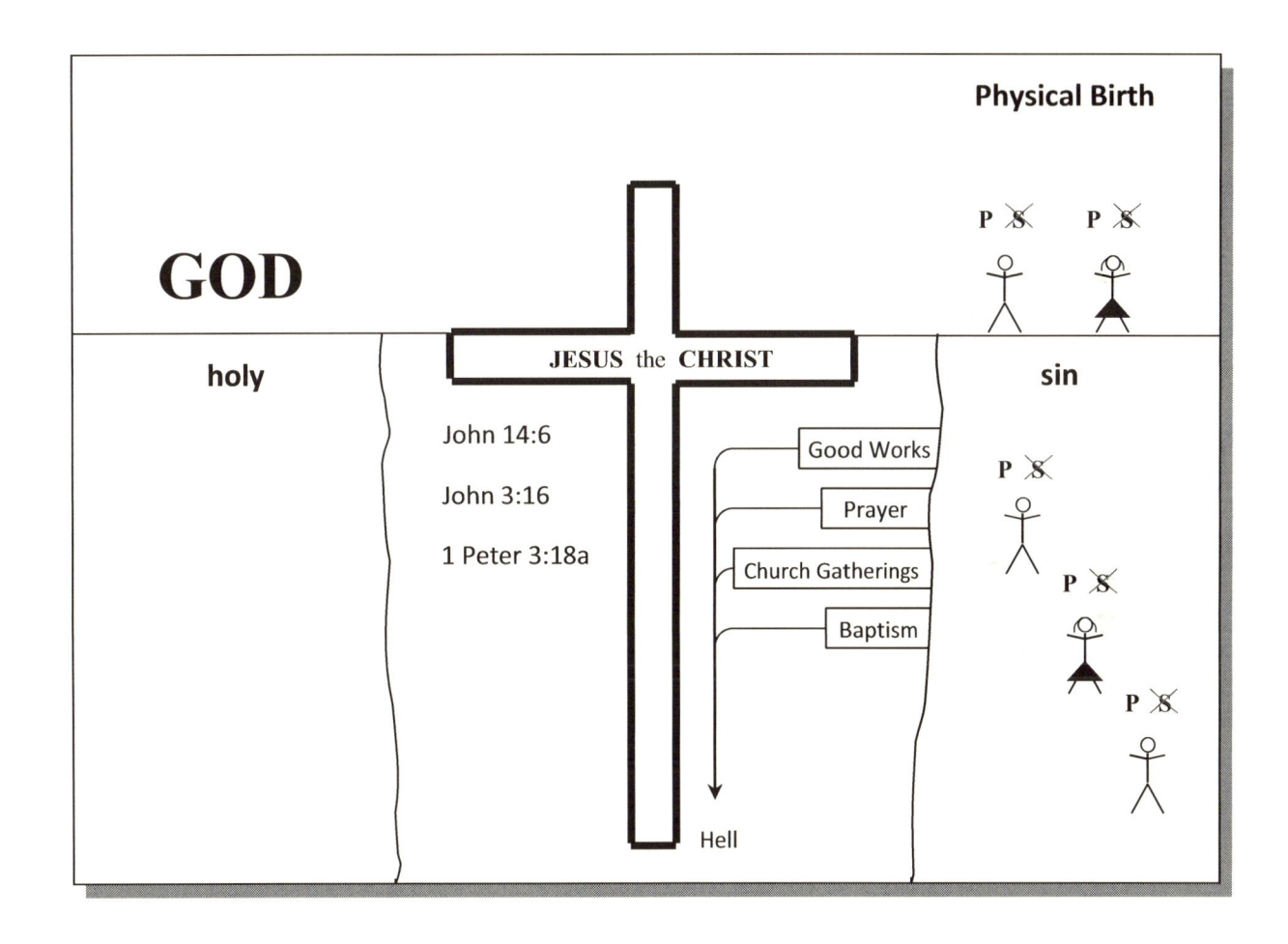

Session 5: *The Way to God*

Physical Birth

GOD

holy

JESUS the CHRIST

John 14:6

John 3:16

1 Peter 3:18a

Good Works

Prayer

Church Gatherings

Baptism

Hell

sin

Session 5: *The Way to God*

Drawing Session 5: *The Way to God*

Write "**John 14:6**" on the left side of the chasm.

Write "**John 3:16**" under "John 14:6"

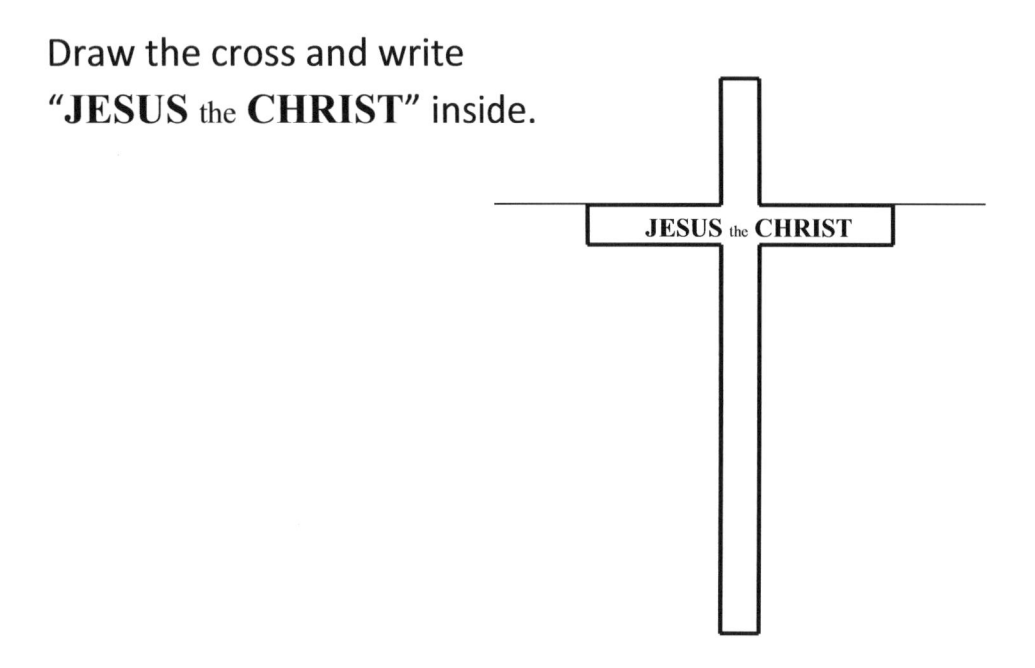

Draw the cross and write
"**JESUS** the **CHRIST**" inside.

Write "**1 Peter 3:18a**" under "John 3:16"

Session 5: *The Way to God*

Questions for Session 5: *The Way to God*

1.0 What did Jesus say concerning the way to God, the truth about God, and true spiritual life? *"Jesus said to him, "I am the way, and the truth, and the life. No one comes to the Father except through me" (first, second, and third paragraph, John 14:6).*

2.1 What did Jesus actually do in order to become the bridge so that we can cross over from spiritual death to spiritual life? *By shedding His blood and dying upon the cross, being buried in the grave, and resurrected the third day according to the scriptures, Jesus became the life-giving savior for mankind (fourth paragraph, 1 Corinthians 15:2-4).*

2.2 Why would Jesus do this? *To obey the Father and do His will (fourth paragraph, Philippians 2:8).*

3.0 Look up in the Bible and write out the verse John 14:6. *"Jesus said to him, "I am the way, and the truth, and the life. No one comes to the Father except through me" (John 14:6).*

4.0 Look up in the Bible and write out the verse John 3:16. *"For God so loved the world, that he gave his only Son, that whoever believes in him should not perish but have eternal life" (John 3:16).*

5.0 Look up in the Bible and write out the verse 1 Peter 3:18. *For Christ also suffered once for sins, the righteous for the unrighteous, that he might bring us to God, being put to death in the flesh but made alive in the spirit..." (1 Peter 3:18).*

Session 6: *Being Born Again*

In this chapter we will explore:
    1). What does it mean to be born again?
    2). How does someone become a child of God?
    3). What is the Tri-unity of God?

When we come to God by having faith in Jesus Christ, we pass from spiritual death to spiritual life. God gives us spiritual life.[49] We now have the highest quality of life (i.e. eternal life) that can never be taken away. One of the passages in the Bible that speaks of this life is 1 John 5:11 and 12, "And this is the testimony, that God gave us eternal life, and this life is in his Son. Whoever has the Son has life; whoever does not have the Son of God does not have life."

In John 3:1-10, the Bible tells us about a man named Nicodemous who came to Jesus to make inquiries of Him. Jesus explained to Nicodemous how he could cross the gulf of separation between him and God. Jesus said, "no one can enter the kingdom of God unless he is born again." Being born again is referencing a second birth. Nicodemous said to Jesus, "How can a man be born when he is old? Can he enter a second time into his mother's womb and be born?" Nicodemous understood the first birth is a physical birth but he was confused because he did not understand that the second birth Jesus was talking about is a spiritual birth. Everyone is born physically alive but spiritually dead. Our physical parents give physical birth but we need our spiritual parent (i.e. God) to give us spiritual birth. The Bible says that when we are united with Christ through faith, we become a new creation. Just like with any birth, when someone is spiritually born they are a born a new little spiritual baby.

There was a man named John the Baptist that came to prepare people for the coming of Jesus.[50] He baptized people in water as he proclaimed, "Repent, for the kingdom of heaven is at hand."[51] Repentance is to have a changed mind. We need to have a new heart which will give us a changed mind.[52] The idea is we need to be

Session 6: *Being Born Again*

spiritually born a new person.[53] John the Baptist said he was baptizing with water, but Jesus was coming and would baptize people with the Holy Spirit.[54] Jesus totally immerses or saturates people with the Holy Spirit so that they are identified with the Holy Spirit. At the moment someone believes (i.e. has faith, trusts, crosses over The Bridge, etc.) they are born again, or become regenerate. Upon regeneration, at that very moment, is when Jesus baptizes them with the Holy Spirit.

Who is the Holy Spirit? Just like the Father is God, and Jesus is God, so the Holy Spirit is God. Christ did not teach there are three Gods; by no means, He clearly taught there is only ONE GOD.[55] But Jesus clearly revealed that the one true God is God the Father; God the Son; and God the Holy Spirit; three Persons eternally coexisting in the Godhead, yet only one true God. Each Person is the exact same in substance, yet distinct in subsistence. This teaching is often known as the Trinity.[56] This is a difficult concept that can only be accepted and truly understood through faith by those that are born again (i.e. regenerate). Jesus gave His followers a command that they are to physically do which creates a symbolic picture of the tri-unity of God (i.e. trinity).

One of the great missions, or things Jesus was to accomplish, was to reveal God's name. At the end of Jesus' incarnate ministry, He said to His Father that He had accomplished all that the Father had sent Him to do. He said that He had perfectly revealed God's name.[57] The idea of revealing a name is to reveal the very essence or complete identity of a person. After Jesus was resurrected from the dead, right before He ascended up into heaven, He commanded His followers to go and help others know and follow His teachings (a follower of Jesus' teachings is called a disciple).[58] And one of the things He commanded His disciples to do was to go and make other disciples. They were to symbolically water baptize them into God's name. The command is to immerse them into the Father, and immerse them into the Son, and immerse them into the Holy Spirit.[59] Three dips yet only one baptism into the name of God. The symbolic Christian water baptism is a picture of a

Session 6: *Being Born Again*

disciple being saturated and identified with the one true God; namely, God the Father, God the Son, and God the Holy Spirit. There are three dips yet only one baptism, just like there are three Persons of the Godhead yet only one true God.

When we are born again, we become what the Bible calls a child of God. This new spiritual relationship is described in John 1:12-13, "But to all who did receive him, who believed in his name, he gave the right to become children of God, who were born, not of blood nor of the will of the flesh nor of the will of man, but of God." To be born again, to become a child of God, someone must receive Jesus and believe in His name. Again, when someone has faith (i.e. trusts, believes, etc.) in Jesus they receive Him. To believe in His name is to believe in the very essence, the true complete identity, of His very being.

What a great gift God has given us – to be part of His family. Through Jesus the Christ, we are adopted by God as His child and experience all the benefits of being a child of the Creator of the universe. Equally amazing is the fact that this newfound relationship with God is not something that will eventually happen. It is a now thing! We are born again and given eternal life at the very moment we believe and receive Christ through faith. We are a new creation and receive a new nature; the nature of our heavenly Father. Though a child of God still has their old sin nature, lives are changed the moment people come to God through Christ as they receive God's nature.[60] Is it any wonder life takes on a new wonderful meaning? Is it any wonder we want to get to know God better through the Bible or share the "Good News" of Jesus Christ with others?

The following diagram illustrates the summary of this chapter: the "Spiritual Birth" at the top left; the people who crossed over The Bridge (i.e. who were born again) are spiritually alive (i.e. no "X" through the "S"); the "Born Again (John 3:1-10)" above the line showing people crossing over the bridge; and the additional verses "1 John 5:11-12 and John 1:12-13.

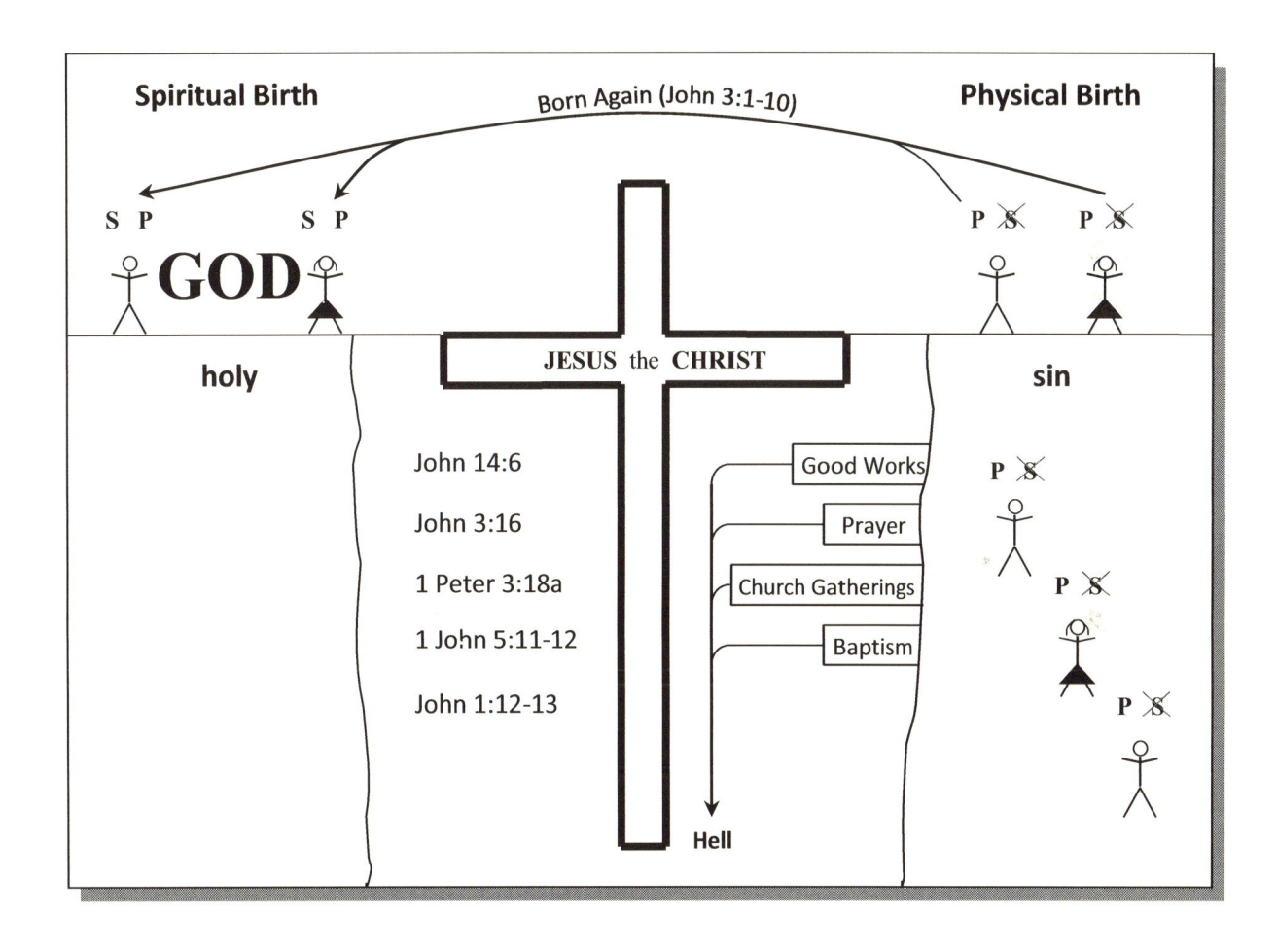

Session 6: *Being Born Again*

Spiritual Birth — Born Again (John 3:1-10) — **Physical Birth**

S P   S P   P S   P S

GOD

holy   sin

JESUS the CHRIST

John 14:6

John 3:16

1 Peter 3:18a

1 John 5:11-12

John 1:12-13

Good Works

Prayer

Church Gatherings

Baptism

Hell

P S

P S

P S

Session 6: *Being Born Again*

Drawing Session 6: *Being Born Again*

Draw the two new stick figures on the other side of the chasm, one on each side next to God. Write an "**S**" for spiritual life and a "**P**" for physical life above each stick figure.

S P   GOD   S P

Draw an arrow from each stick figure on the "Physical Birth" side over to the "Spiritual Birth" side.

Write "**Spiritual Birth**" in the upper left-hand corner.

Write "**1 John 5:11-12**" under "1 Peter 3:18a."

Write "**Born Again (John 3:1-10)**" on top of the line connecting the stick figures.

Write "**John 1:12-13**" under "1 John 5:11-12."

Session 6: *Being Born Again*

Questions for Session 6: *Being Born Again*

1.1 According to 1 John 5:11-12, if someone has the Son (i.e. Jesus the Christ) what else do they have? *Whoever has the Son has life... (first paragraph, 1 John 5:11-12).*

1.2 According to 1 John 5:11-12, if someone does not have the Son of God (i.e. Jesus the Christ) what else do they not have? *Whoever does not have the Son of God does not have life... (first paragraph, 1 John 5:11-12).*

2.0 What happens at the very moment when someone becomes a child of God (i.e. believes in Jesus, receives Jesus, has faith or trusts in Jesus, accepts Jesus, crosses over The Bridge, becomes regenerate, born again, saved, etc.)? *They are spiritually born again as a new person, with a new heart, and new mind (i.e. they become regenerate). Jesus baptizes them into the Holy Spirit. They become part of God's family. They now have eternal life. They become a new creation and receive a new nature; the nature of their Heavenly Father (third and sixth paragraph).*

3.1 The very essence or name of God is Trinitarian. God is ___three___ Persons yet only ___one___ true God. *(fourth and fifth paragraph).*

3.2 Who are the three Persons of the one true God? *God the Father, God the Son, and God the Holy Spirit (fourth and fifth paragraph, Matthew 28:19).*

4.0 **True** or **(False)** When someone becomes born again they become a new creation with the nature of their Heavenly Father; therefore, they will never sin anymore and life will be easy and they will be happy all the time. *The first part of this questions is definitely true; however, the last part of this question is false. Unfortunately, the Christian also still possesses the sin nature until death or the coming of the Lord (seventh paragraph, Romans 7:13-20).*

Session 7: *God's Speed*

Eternal life is a gift! The Bible says, "For by grace you have been saved through faith. And this is not your own doing; it is the gift of God, not a result of works, so that no one may boast."[61] Receiving eternal life is not based on what we do, but rather on what God has done. God the Father has sent His Son. God the Son has sacrificially died on the cross and raised the third day. God the Holy Spirit gives us new birth through faith in Jesus the Christ.

The gift of eternal life is something no one deserves and which no one can repay. There is nothing anyone can do to merit God's grace – it is a gift! Grace is God's unmerited favor given to man. It is a gift given through faith. Only those who have received the gift of eternal life through faith in Christ can serve God through good works. When we are given this new life, we have a relationship with the Father and can actually talk with Him (i.e. prayer). We are part of His family (i.e. His church). We are spiritually baptized into the one true God.

When we receive the gift of eternal life we are saved – saved from the deserved wrath of God. "For all have sinned"[62] and deserve, or have earned, eternal death.[63] "But God shows his love for us in that while we were still sinners, Christ died for us."[64] Someone has to pay the due penalty of sin to a just and holy God. We have one of two choices: either we can receive the penalty for our sin (this yields eternal death and damnation) or we can allow Christ to receive the penalty for our personal sin (this yields eternal life). The Bible says every knee will bow and tongue confess Jesus is Lord.[65] You can either do this now through faith and receive eternal life **or** you will do this after you physically die and experience the second death.

We are all at one spiritual place or another as we travel through this temporal journey we call life. As I have said, I am just one beggar telling another beggar where I found bread. If you can help find some more bread, I would be appreciative. If there is anything I could do to help you on your journey, I would be willing and honored. May we all have God's speed as we travel on this journey to the everlasting!

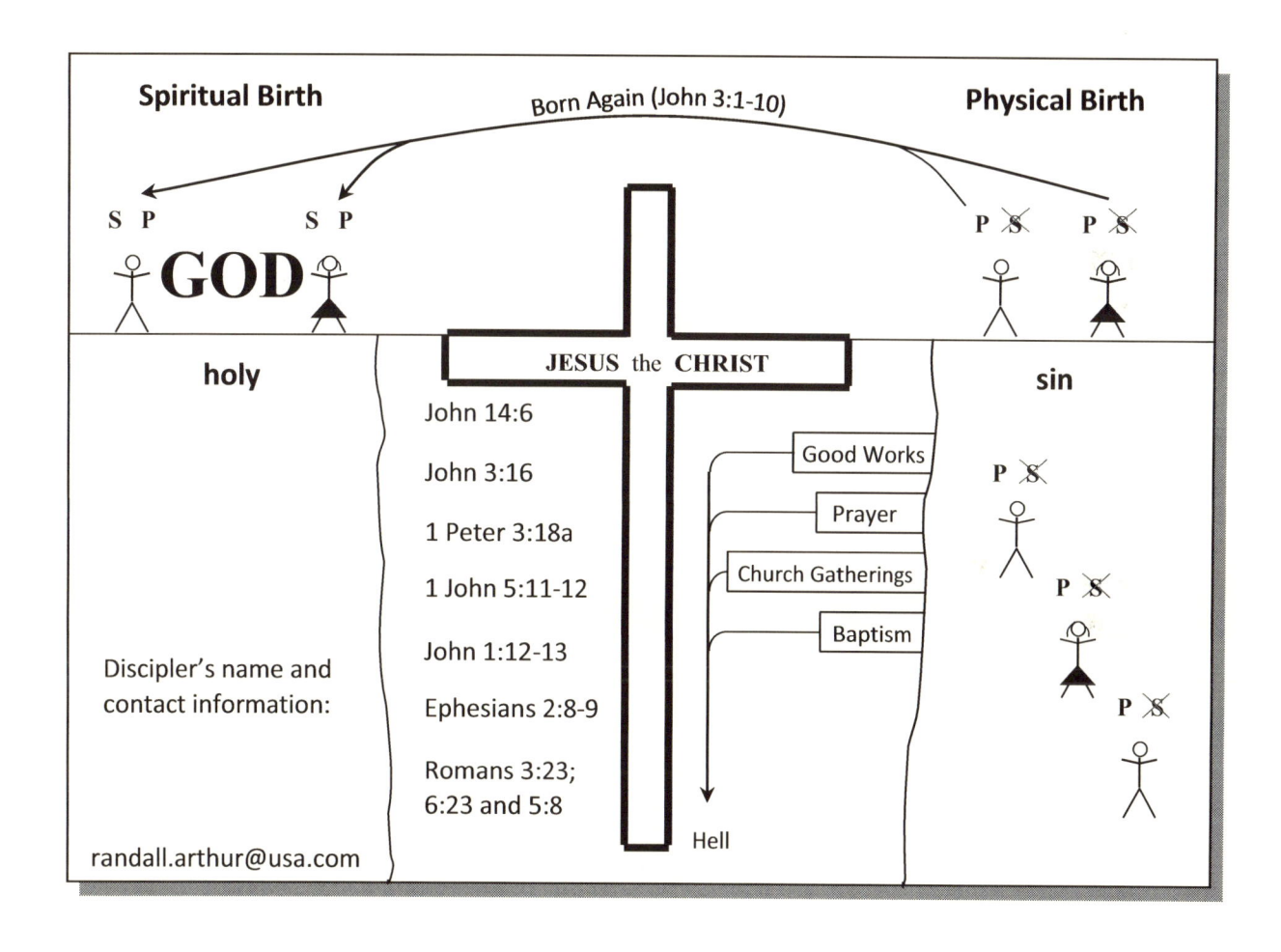

Session 7: *God's Speed*

Spiritual Birth — Born Again (John 3:1-10) — **Physical Birth**

S P   S P   P S̶   P S̶

GOD

holy   JESUS the CHRIST   sin

John 14:6

John 3:16   Good Works   P S̶

1 Peter 3:18a   Prayer

1 John 5:11-12   Church Gatherings   P S̶

John 1:12-13   Baptism

Discipler's name and
contact information: Ephesians 2:8-9   P S̶

Romans 3:23;
6:23 and 5:8

randall.arthur@usa.com   Hell

39

Session 7: *God's Speed*

So what's next? If you are a child of God, then the simplest answer to that question is to follow Jesus. But what exactly does it mean to follow Jesus? Jesus said that just as the Father has sent Him into the world, He is now sending us. The Father sent Jesus to glorify the Father by making Him known. The way to know the Father is by knowing Jesus. So how do you get to know Jesus? The only way to know Jesus is through the Holy Spirit revealing Him to us through the truth of the Scriptures. Here is a summary on how this all works:

- The purpose of our life is to glorify God. The way we glorify God is getting to know Him (i.e. having a restored relationship with Him) and helping others get to know Him.
- The only way to know Jesus is by having the Holy Spirit reveal Him to us through the truth of the Scripture.
- The only way to know the Father is by knowing Jesus.
- As the Father is made known, God is glorified.
- As we help people get to know God through the truth of the Scriptures, God is made known and therefore glorified.

So the next step is to learn how to properly interact, study, and interpret the Bible so you can get to know and glorify God. We have designed a discipleship curriculum to help in this process. If you would like more information on these materials, please do not hesitate to contact us.

We are all at one spiritual place or another as we travel through this temporal journey we call life. As I have said, I am just one beggar telling another beggar where I found bread. If you can help me find some more bread, I would be appreciative. If there is anything I could do to help you on your journey, I would be willing and honored: randall.arthur@usa.com. God's speed on your spiritual journey!

Scripture Footnotes

1. John 14:21
2. Matthew 7:15-20 with James 3:11-12
3. Romans 3:23 with 5:12, 18-19
4. Leviticus 11:44-45 with Hebrews 13:8 and Revelation 1:8
5. Genesis 1
6. Genesis 2:7
7. Genesis 1:27
8. Genesis 2:8
9. Genesis 2:16-17
10. Genesis 1:29-30; 2:10-11 with 2:15
11. Genesis 2:20-22
12. Genesis 3:2-3
13. Genesis 3:6-7
14. Romans 5:12
15. Romans 8:3-17
16. Romans 14:23
17. Isaiah 14:12-15
18. Luke 10:18
19. Romans 5:12 with Romans 6:23
20. Titus 1:2
21. Matthew 10:28
22. James 2:26
23. Romans 6:19 with Genesis 6:5
24. John 8:34 with Romans 6:19
25. Genesis 3:23-24
26. Genesis 3:17-18 with Romans 5:17
27. Isaiah 64:6
28. 1 Samuel 16:7
29. Romans 1:18-25
30. John 3:36 with Revelation 20:10, 14-15
31. 1 Timothy 2:3-4
32. 1 John 4:8-10
33. Psalm 14:1, 53:1

34. John 14:6
35. John 3:16
36. John 8:32
37. John 17:3
38. John 10:10
39. 1 Corinthians 15:2-4
40. John 10:31
41. Philippians 2:11
42. Luke 18:27
43. Philippians 2:8
44. Hebrews 4:15
45. John 1:1, 14
46. Luke 1:27, 34
47. 1 Peter 3:18a
48. Romans 5:7-8
49. Romans 4:17
50. John 1:6-7
51. Matthew 4:17
52. Ezekiel 36:26-27
53. 2 Corinthians 5:17
54. Luke 3:16
55. Deuteronomy 6:4
56. Matthew 3:16-17
57. John 17:4-6
58. Matthew 28:16-20
59. Matthew 28:19
60. Romans 7:13-20
61. Ephesians 2:8-9
62. Romans 3:23
63. Romans 6:23
64. Romans 5:8
65. Philippians 2:10-11

Made in the USA
Charleston, SC
02 March 2014